Carmine Caruso

a sequel to... musical calisthenics for brass

Compiled by Dominic Derasse

ISBN 978-1-4950-7473-8

7777 W. BLUEMOUND RD. P.O.BOX 13819 MILWAUKEE, WI 53213

In Australia Contact:
Hal Leonard Australia Pty. Ltd.
4 Lentara Court
Cheltenham, Victoria, 3192 Australia
Email: ausadmin@halleonard.com.au

Visit Hal Leonard Online at
www.halleonard.com

PREFACE

I studied with Carmine between October 1979 and May 1980. For the duration of going through his book *Musical Calisthenics for Brass* (MCFB), I would see him once a week. As we progressed, it turns out Carmine had many more exercises to share with me, and by February 1980, I decided I wanted to see him twice a week. I have been teaching Mr. Caruso's method ever since 1980. Recently, when Hugo Moreno and Chris Scanlon finished MCFB, we were discussing the extended exercises. This discussion resulted in the idea of putting these extended exercises into a book. This book is the result of our collaboration.

This sequel is a continuation of MCFB, and should be started only after the completion of Carmine's original method.

In approaching these exercises, whether this book or the original MCFB, it is extremely important to fully comprehend Carmine's philosophy. One must therefore follow all remarks and rules outlined in Mr. Caruso's original book. The most important thing I learned from Carmine was how to teach myself. In studying his method, each pupil should seek the same goal.

The five principles based in Zen: **Coordination, Synchronization, Conditioned Reflex, Second Nature,** and the **Instrument Becoming an Extension of the Body** must be well understood and followed, as well as the four rules that apply to playing the exercises in MCFB and in this book:

- Tap your foot.

- Keep the mouthpiece in contact with your lips throughout each exercise.

- Breathe through the nose.

- Keep the blow steady.

It is my intent with this book to continue Mr. Caruso's legacy. I hope anyone undertaking the study of his method can benefit from it as much as I have. I continue to learn every day both in performance and in sharing with fellow musicians who come to me for input on Mr. Caruso's philosophy and method.

Dominic Derasse
March 2016

dominic@dominicderasse.com

MY TRIBUTE TO CARMINE

I have had a few mentors in my musical life, but the one I credit most is Carmine Caruso. When I had the privilege of studying with Mr. Caruso in 1979-80, I had no idea how my life would change. His teachings and philosophy not only enabled me to pursue the career I wanted as a musician playing the trumpet, but also transformed my life as a person.

The biggest lesson I learned from Carmine was how to teach myself. The "Five Steps" involved in his teachings, based in Zen, enabled me to understand how the body and mind function in a way I had never witnessed or even imagined before meeting him. I discovered that these Steps could be applied to anything one wants to accomplish in life – musical or otherwise.

It therefore made sense that even though Mr. Caruso played clarinet, saxophone, violin and piano (he was successful in teaching any instrumentalist), he became mostly known for helping brass players and, more specifically, trumpet players.

By the time I met Carmine, I had already graduated from the Paris Conservatory and was considered an accomplished musician, but still felt I was far from having the physical attributes necessary to bring my trumpet playing to the high level I was seeking. Caruso's techniques, focusing on the physical aspects of playing an instrument, showed me the way to develop the physical requirements necessary to playing my instrument and subsequently the technical requirements as well. All to better serve the *music* I wanted to play.

Not a day that goes by, 36 years later, without him being directly involved in my life, because I still use his routine daily. There also is no greater sense of purpose, 29 years after his passing, than to try to continue and perpetuate his legacy by sharing his teachings with new generations.

Forever grateful, Carmine!

Dominic Derasse
April 2016

2

Reminder: All the rules from *Musical Calisthenics for Brass* apply to all the excercises in this book.

1. **Tap your foot ♩ = 60**
2. **Keep the mouthpiece in contact with the lips throughout each exercise.**
3. **Breathe through the nose.**
4. **Keep the blow steady.**

Lesson 1

Exercise 1: Six Notes

Measure 19 to the end is an optional 8vb.

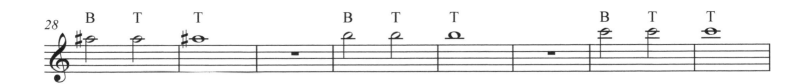

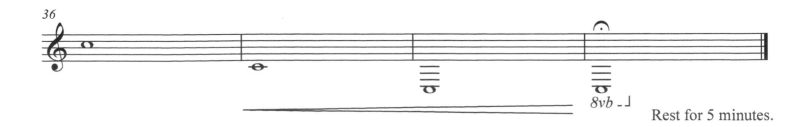

Rest for 5 minutes.

Exercise 2: Intervals in 9ths

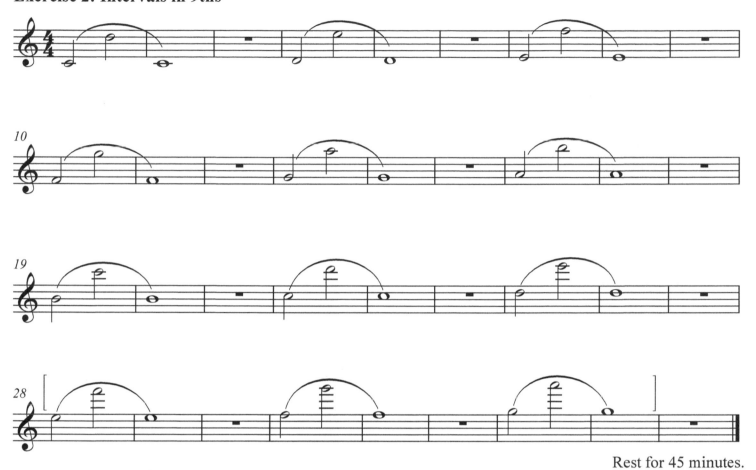

Rest for 45 minutes.

As in MCFB, play the interval exercises as high as you can go,
pause 8-10 seconds, pick up where you left off and continue again
as high as you can go. The three reasons for which you will stop are:

1. No sound comes out.
2. Sound comes out, but you are on the wrong partial.
3. You feel dizzy.

On 1. and 2. make sure to keep trying throughout
the full eight beats of the particular interval.
It is at after this point that you
take the 45 minute break.

4

Lesson 2

Play Excercise 1, followed by 5 minutes of rest.
Play Excercise 2, followed by 15 minutes of rest.

Exercise 3: Harmonics

Rest for 15 minutes.

Exercise 4: Intervals in 10ths

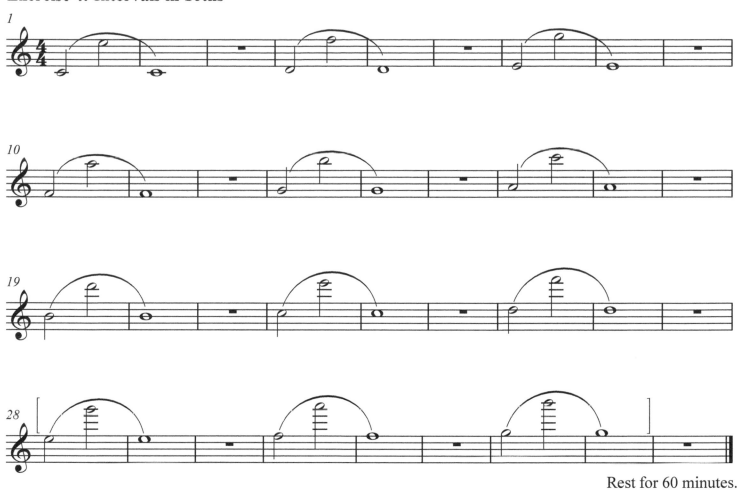

Rest for 60 minutes.

Note: During the rest time, it is recommended that you do not play anything.

As you progress through this book, as in Carmine's MCFB,
the goal through each lesson is to add more exercises
and reduce the rest times so that your "workout" will still
fit within approximately a one-hour time frame.

Lesson 3

Play Excercise 1 and rest for 5 minutes.
Play Excercise 2 and rest for 8 minutes.
Play Excercise 3 and rest for 8 minutes.
Play Excercise 4 and rest for 8 minutes.

Exercise 5: Intervals in 11ths

Rest for 8 minutes.

Reminder:
The Caruso rules apply only to the exercises in this book.
With the exception of rule #4, they should not be applied to
your other playing. The excercises in this book, as in
Carmine's MCFB, are purely calisthenic.

Exercise 6: Intervals in 9ths – Soft Loud Soft

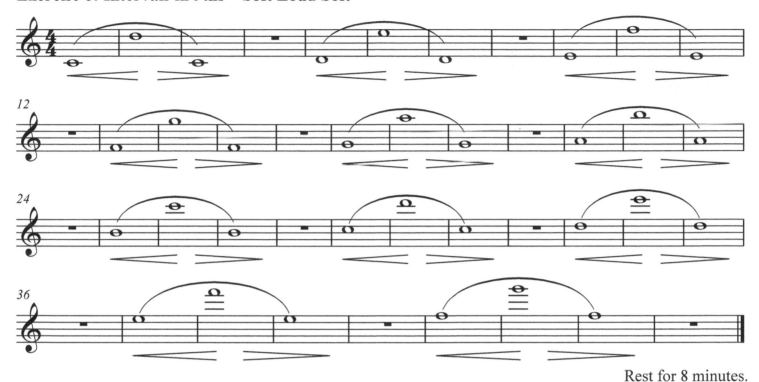

Rest for 8 minutes.

Play the Soft-Loud-Soft (SLS) exercises as high as you can go, pause 8-10 seconds,
pickup where you left off and continue again as high as you can go.
The three reason for which you will stop are:

1. No sound comes out
2. Sound comes out, but you are on the wrong partial.
3. You feel dizzy.

On 1. and 2., make sure to keep trying throughout the full 12 beats of the
particular interval. It is at after this point that you take the break.

Exercise 7: Lip Flexibility 1

Rest for 60 minutes.

8

Lesson 4

Play Exercise 1 and rest for 3 minutes.
Play Exercise 2 and rest for 5 minutes.
Play Exercise 3 and rest for 5 minutes.
Play Exercise 4 and rest for 5 minutes.
Play Exercise 5 and rest for 5 minutes.
Play Exercise 6 and rest for 5 minutes.
Play Exercise 7 and rest for 5 minutes.

Exercise 8: Intervals in 12ths

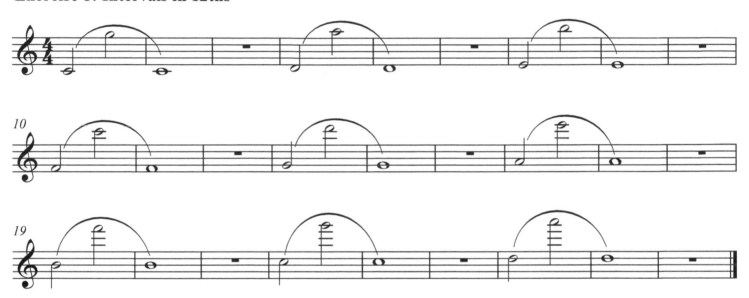

Rest for 5 minutes.

Exercise 9: Intervals in 10ths – SLS

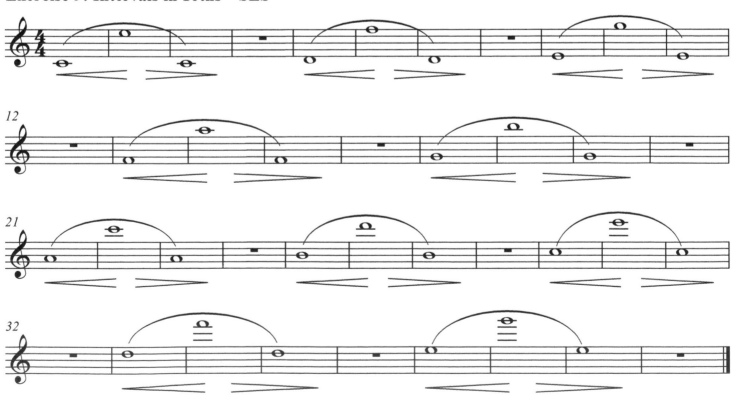

Rest for 60 minutes.

Lesson 5

Play Exercise 1 and rest for 1 minute.
Play Exercise 2 and rest for 3 minutes.
Play Exercise 3 and rest for 3 minutes.
Play Exercise 4 and rest for 3 minutes.
Play Exercise 5 and rest for 3 minutes.
Play Exercise 6 and rest for 3 minutes.
Play Exercise 7 and rest for 3 minutes.
Play Exercise 8 and rest for 3 minutes.
Play Exercise 9 and rest for 3 minutes.

Exercise 10: Intervals in 13ths

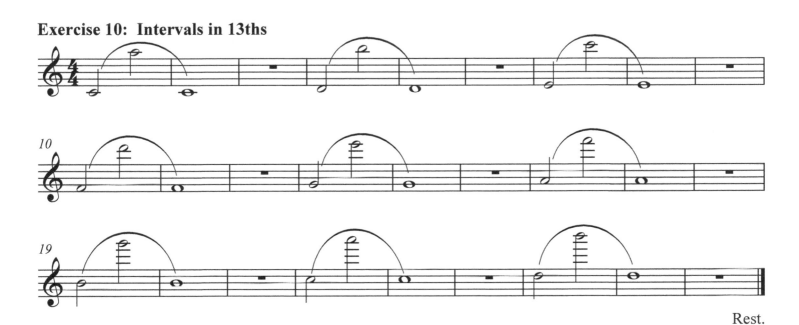

Rest.

Exercise 11: Intervals in 11ths – SLS

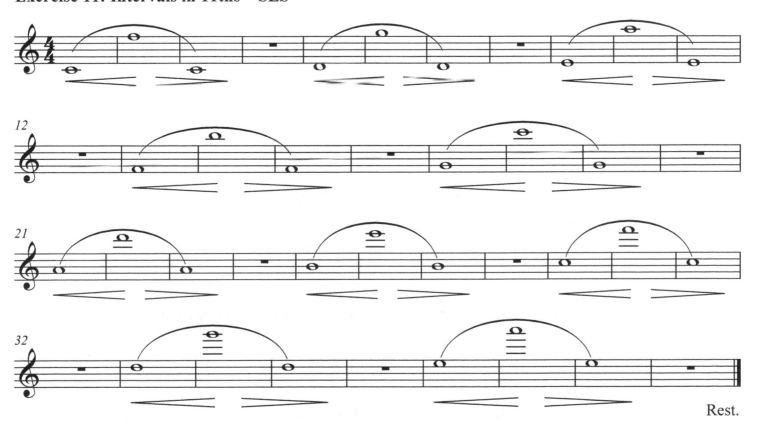

Rest.

Exercise 12: Lip Flexibility 2

Exercise 13: Intervals in 9ths – Loud Soft Loud

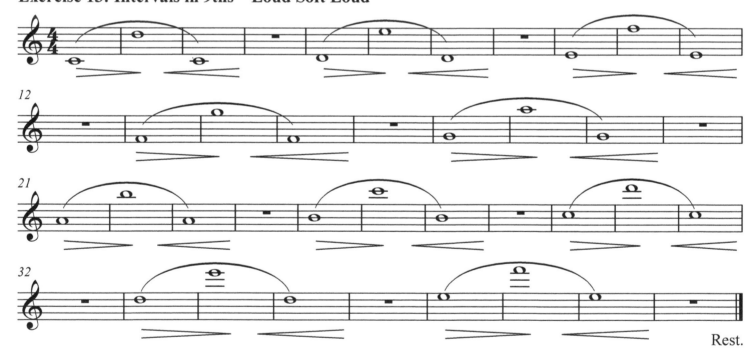

As in MCFB, play the Loud-Soft-Loud (LSL) exercises as high as you can go,
pause 8-10 seconds, pick up where you left off and continue the exercise
as high as you can go. The three reasons for which you will stop are:

1. No sound comes out.
2. Sound comes out, but you are on the wrong partial.
3. You feel dizzy.

On 1. and 2., make sure to keep trying throughout
the full 12 beats of the particular interval.

Exercise 14: Pedals

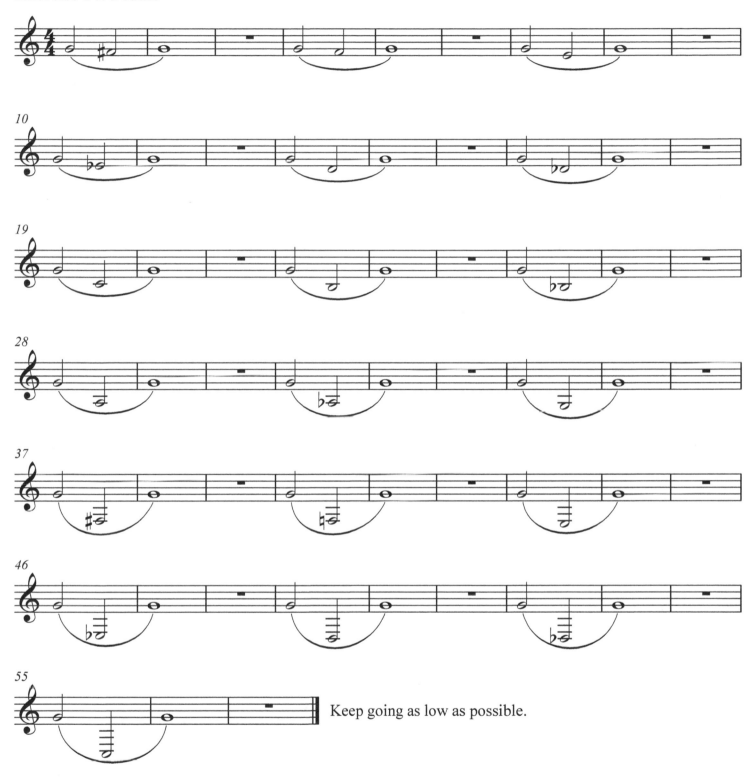

Keep going as low as possible.

Always play the chromatic sequences after the pedal exercise.

Exercise 14a: Chromatics – Expand outward as needed.

Rest for 60 minutes.

Lesson 6

Play Exercise 1 and rest for 1 minute.
Play Exercise 2 and rest for 2 minutes.
Play Exercise 3 and rest for 2 minutes.
Play Exercise 4 and rest for 2 minutes.
Play Exercise 5 and rest for 2 minutes.
Play Exercise 6 and rest for 2 minutes.
Play Exercise 7 and rest for 2 minutes.
Play Exercise 8 and rest for 2 minutes.
Play Exercise 9 and rest for 2 minutes.
Play Exercise 10 and rest for 2 minutes.
Play Exercise 11 and rest for 2 minutes.
Play Exercise 12 and rest for 2 minutes.
Play Exercise 13 and rest for 2 minutes.
Play Exercise 14 and rest for 2 minutes.

Exercise 15: Intervals in 14ths

Rest.

Exercise 16: Intervals in 12ths – SLS

Rest.

Exercise 17: Lip Flexibility 3

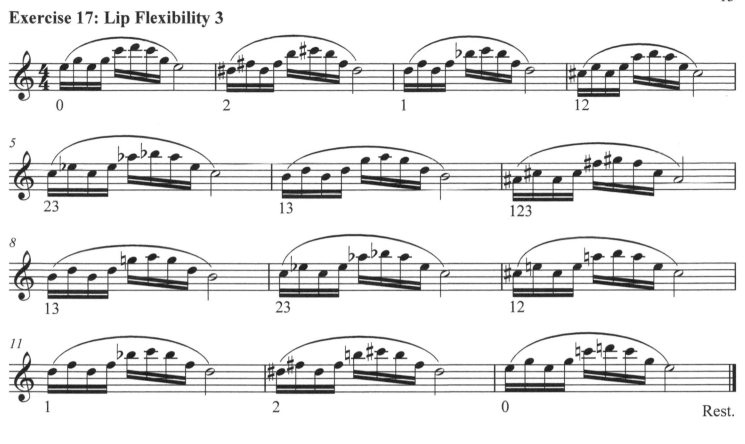

Exercise 18: Intervals in 10ths – LSL

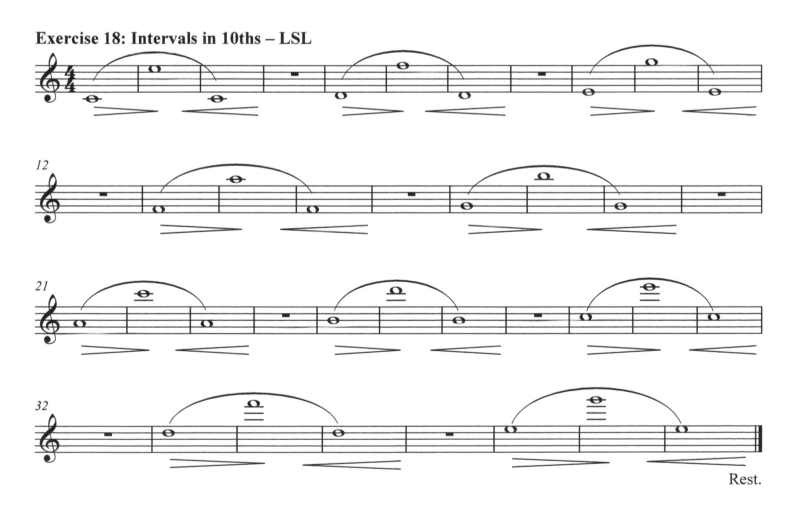

Rest.

Exercise 19: Pedal 2

Play any pedals exercise from MCFB; for example, Exercise 34 on page 37.

14

Lesson 7

Play all of the preceeding exercises with one minute's rest in between, or a period of rest you deem necessary.

Exercise 20: Intervals in Double Octaves

Rest.

Exercise 21: Intervals in 13ths – SLS

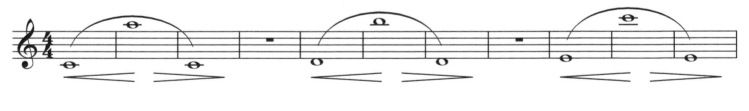

Rest.

Exercise 22: Lip Flexibility 4

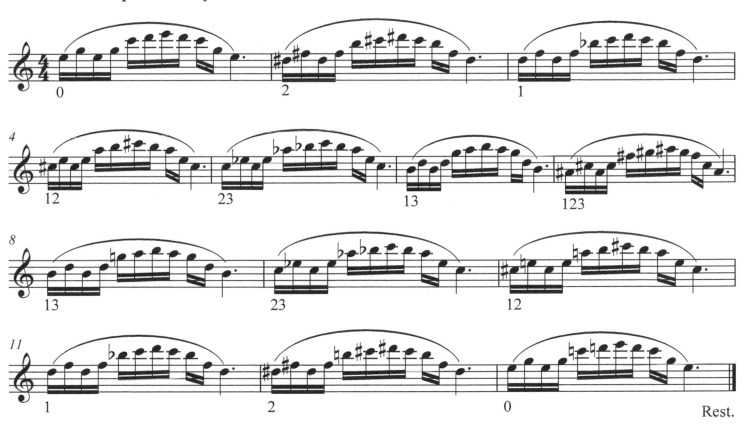

Exercise 23: Intervals in 11ths – LSL

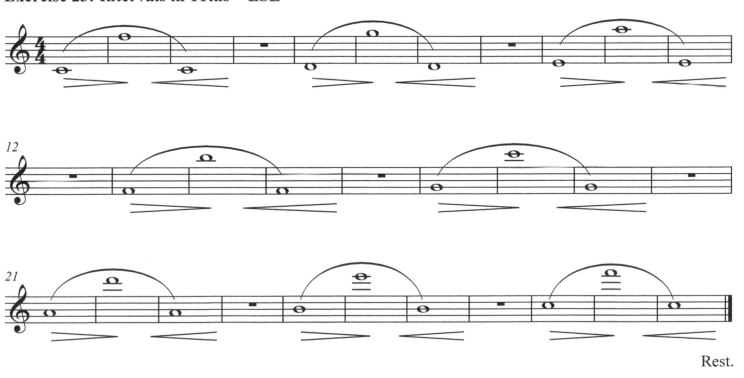

Rest.

Exercise 24: Pedals
Play any pedals exercise from MCFB.

Lesson 8

Exercise 1: Six Notes
Choose 1 Regular Interval (example: Monday – 9ths, Tuesday – 10ths, etc.)
Exercise 3: Harmonics
All subsequent Exercises except regular intervals

Exercise 25: Scales 1 – C major / A minor

Expand above G as your abilities develop.
Practice both slurred and tongued.

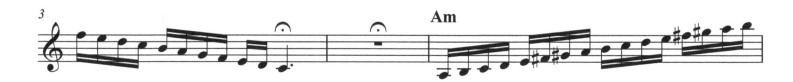

Rest.

Exercise 26: Intervals in 14ths – SLS

Rest.

Exercise 27: Lip Flexibility 5

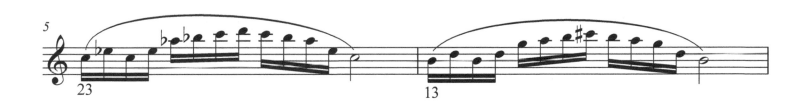

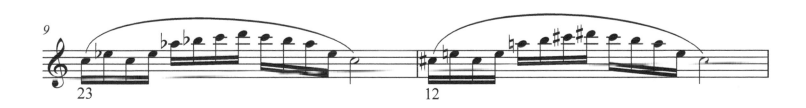

Rest.

Lesson 9

Exercise 1: Six Notes
Choose 1 Regular Interval (example: Monday – 9ths, Tuesday – 10ths, etc.)
Exercise 3: Harmonics
All subsequent Exercises except regular intervals

Exercise 28: Intervals in 12ths – LSL

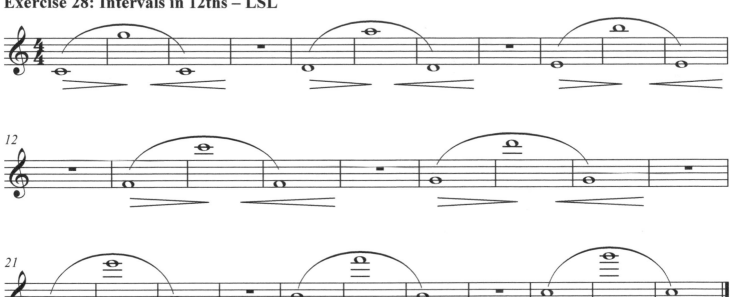

Play Pedal exercise.
Rest.

Exercise 29: Scales 2 – F major / D minor

Rest.

Exercise 30: Intervals in Double Octaves – SLS

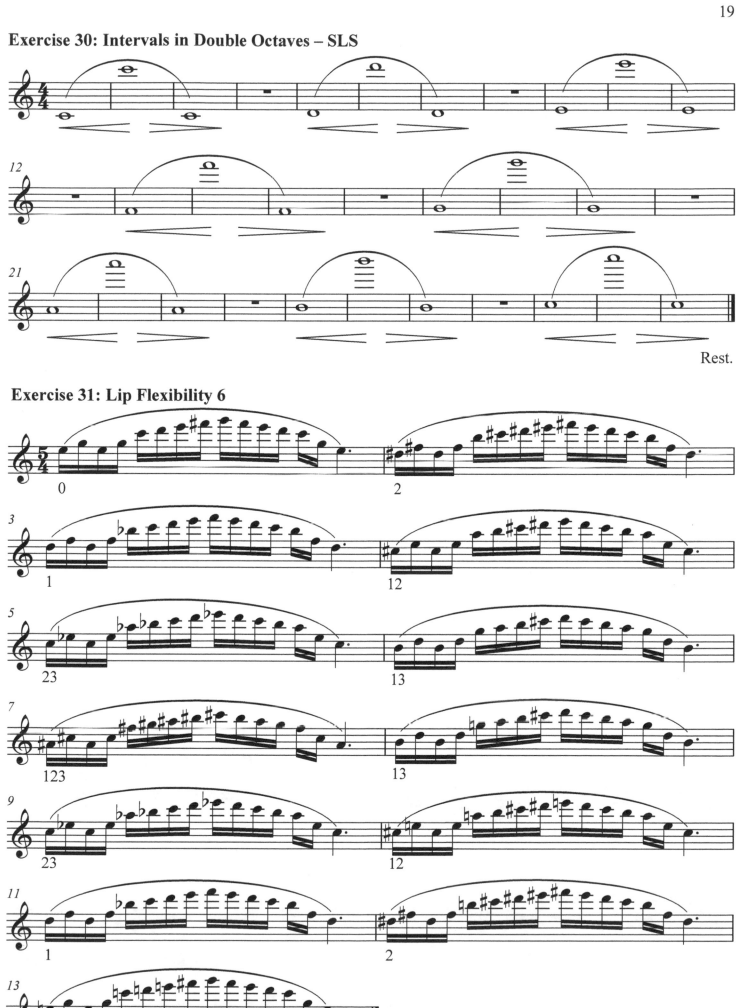

Rest.

Exercise 31: Lip Flexibility 6

Rest.

Exerise 32: Intervals in 13ths – LSL

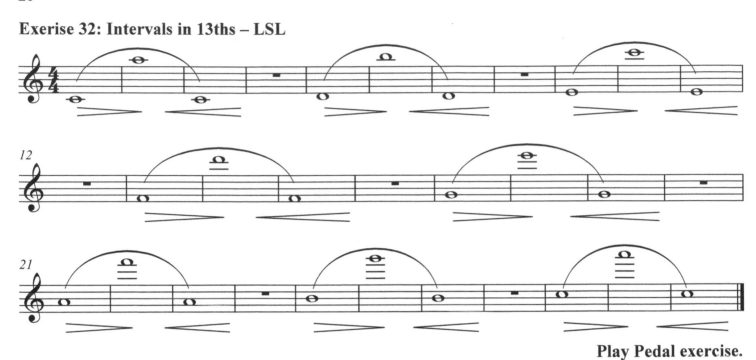

Play Pedal exercise.
Rest.

Lesson 10

Exercise 1: Six Notes
Choose 1 Regular Interval (example: Monday – 11ths, Tuesday – 12ths, etc.)
Exercise 3: Harmonics
Choose 1 SLS Interval (example: Monday – 9ths, Tuesday – 10ths, etc.)
All subsequent Exercises except regular & SLS intervals.

Exercise 33: Expanding Chromatic 1

Exercise 34: Scales 3 – B♭ major / G minor

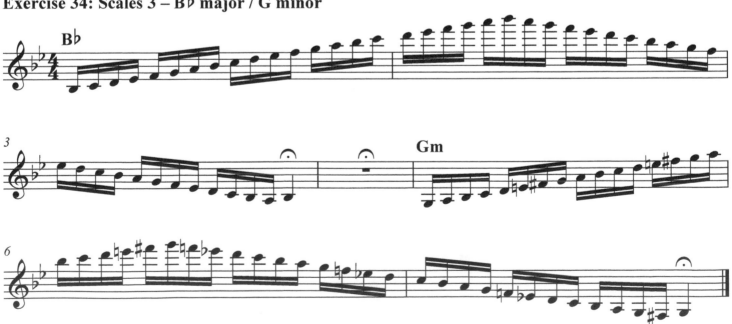

Exercise 35: Developed Intervals in 3rds

Alternate between combinations of tonguing and slurring.

Articulation examples

Exercise 36: Arpeggios 1 – C major / A minor

Alternate slurring and tonguing. The repeats are optional.

Exercise 37: Intervals in 14ths – LSL

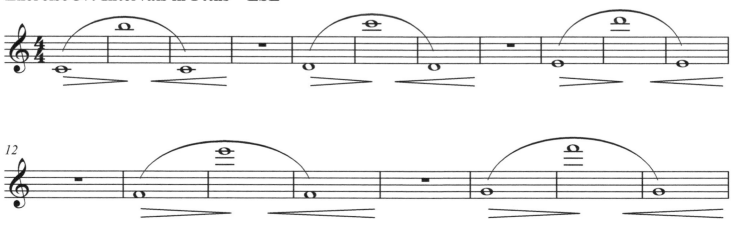

Play Pedal exercise.

Exercise 38: Lip Flexibility 7

Exercise 39: Expanding Chromatic 2

Lesson 11

Exercise 1: Six Notes
Choose 1 Regular Interval (example: Monday – 11ths, Tuesday – 12ths, etc.)
Exercise 3: Harmonics
Choose 1 SLS Interval (example: Monday – 9ths, Tuesday – 10ths, etc.)
All subsequent Exercises except regular and SLS intervals.

Exercise 40: Scales 4 – E♭ major / C minor

Exercise 41: Developed Intervals in 4ths

Exercise 42: Arpeggios 2 – F major / D minor

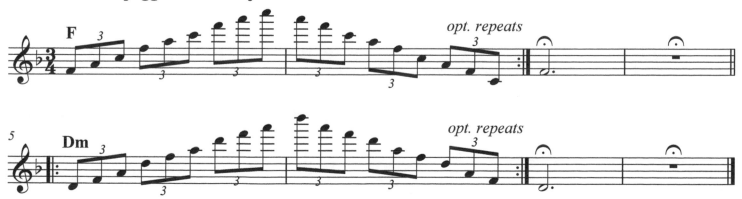

Exercise 43: Tongued Intervals in 2nds

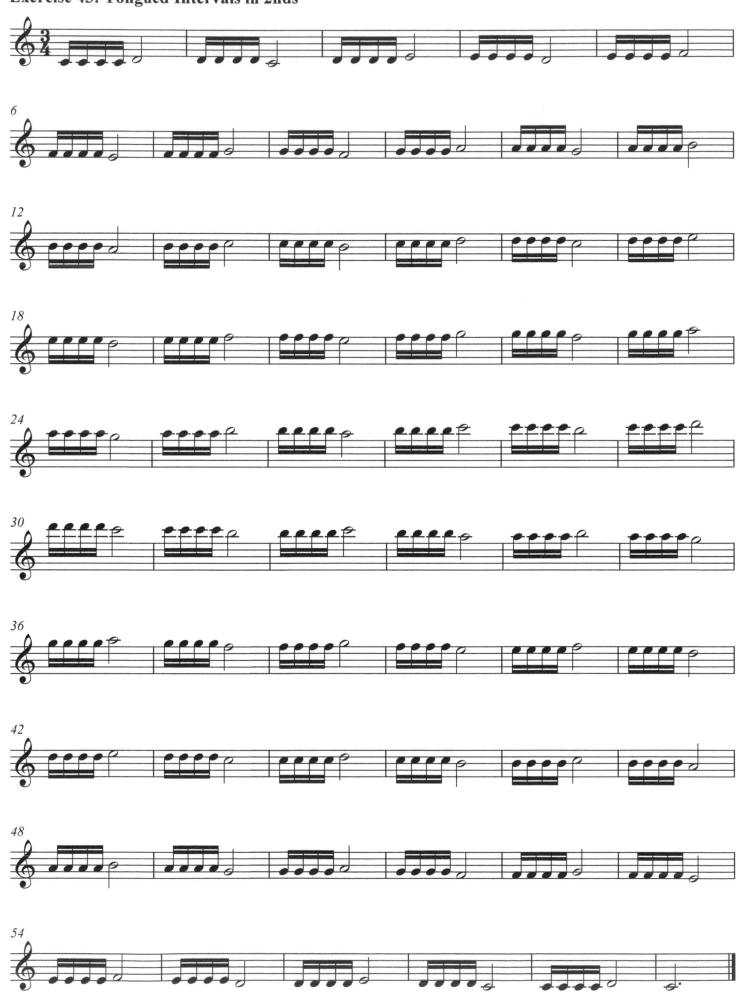

Exercise 44: Intervals in Double Octaves – LSL

Play a Pedal Exercise.

Exercise 45: Lip Flexibility 8

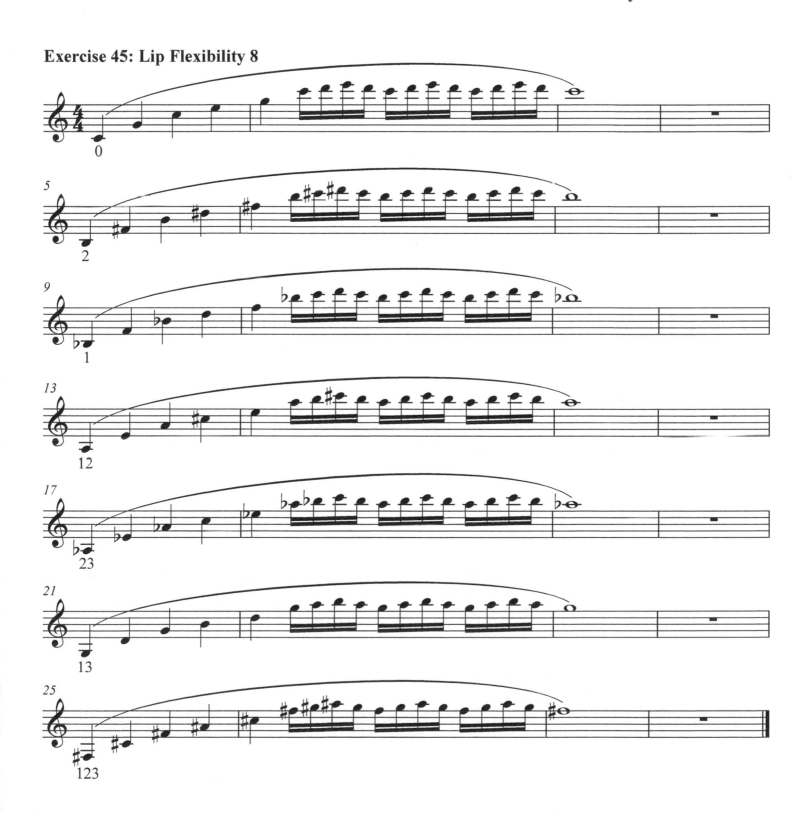

Exercise 46: Expanding Chromatic 3

Lesson 12

Review Chart
Exercise 1: Six Notes
Choose 1 Regular Interval (example: Monday – 13ths, Tuesday – 14ths, etc.)
Exercise 3: Harmonics
Choose 1 SLS Interval (example: Monday – 11ths, Tuesday – 12ths, etc.)
Insert Lip Flexibility 1 (Exercise 7, page 10)
Choose 1 LSL Interval (example: Monday – 9ths, Tuesday – 10ths, etc.)
All subsequent Exercises except regular, SLS, and LSL intervals.

Exercise 47: Scales 5 – A♭ major / F minor

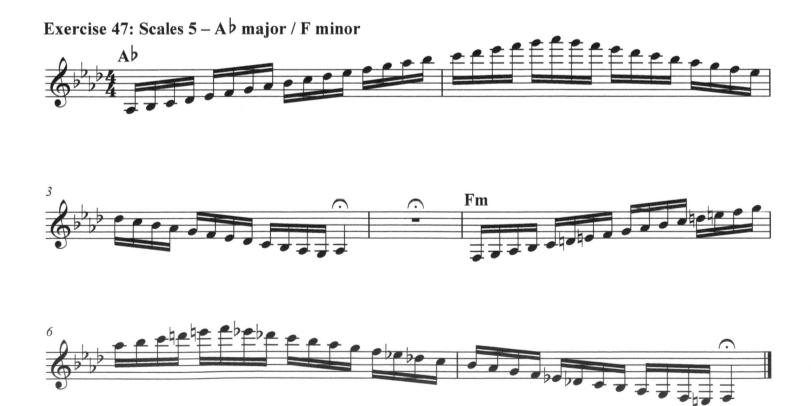

Exercise 48: Developed Intervals in 5ths

Exercise 49: Arpeggios 3 – B♭ major / G minor

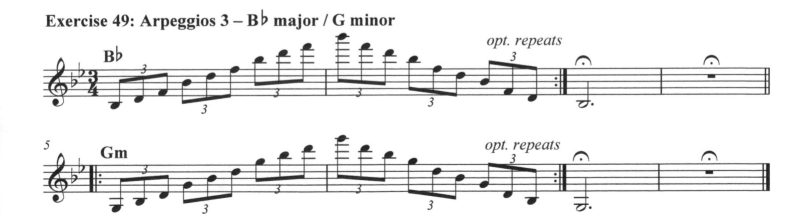

30

Exercise 50: Tongued Intervals in 3rds

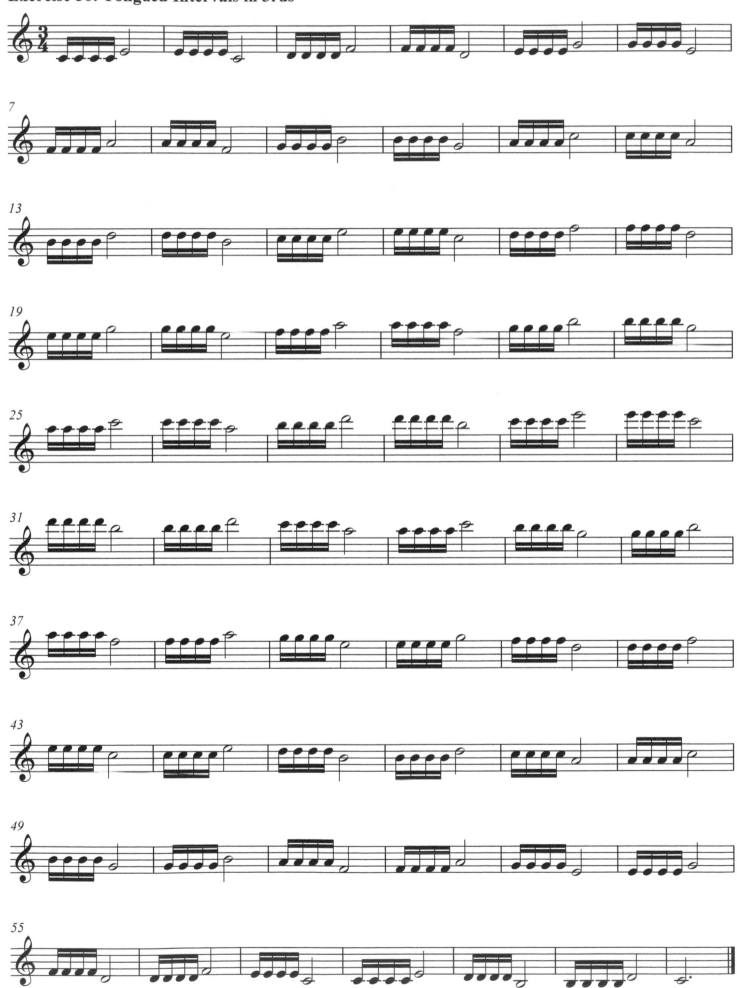

Exercise 51: Lip Flexibility 9

Exercise 52: Subtone 1

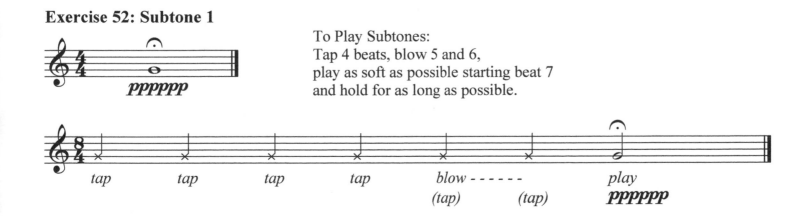

To Play Subtones:
Tap 4 beats, blow 5 and 6,
play as soft as possible starting beat 7
and hold for as long as possible.

Exercise 53 : Expanding Chromatic 4

Lesson 13

Follow **Review Chart** from Lesson 12 (page 28).

Exercise 54: Scales 6 – D♭ major / B♭ minor

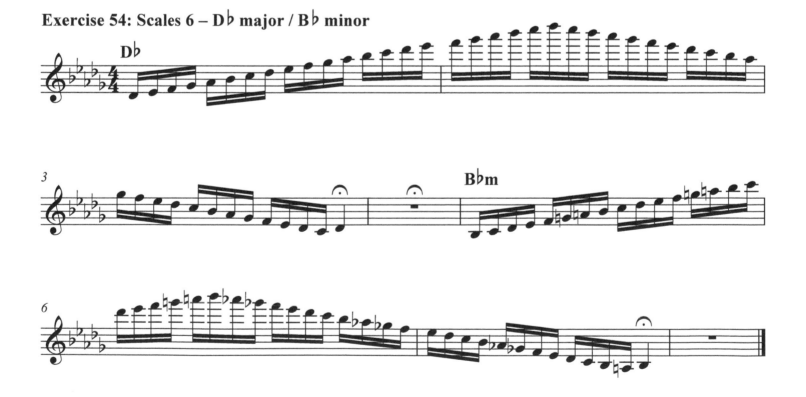

Exercise 55: Developed Intervals in 6ths

Exercise 56: Arpeggios 4 – E♭ major / C minor

Exercise 57: Tongued Intervals in 4ths

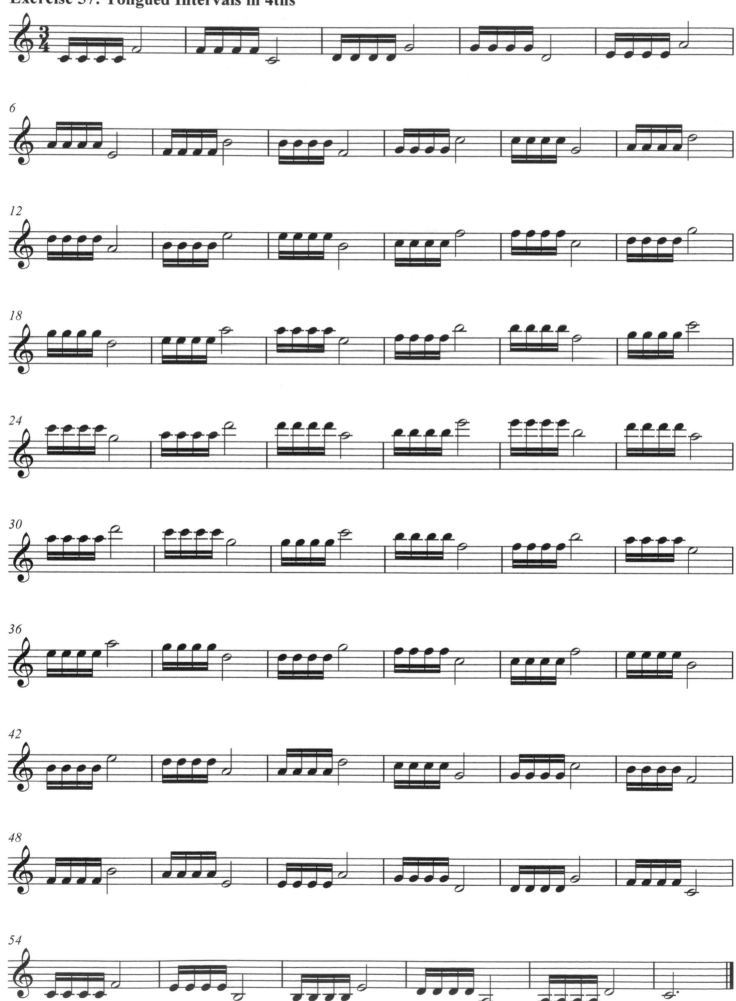

Exercise 58: Subtone 2

Play in the same manner as Subtone 1.

Exercise 59: Expanding Chromatic 5

Lesson 14

Review Chart (page 28)

Exercise 60: Scales 7 – G♭ major / E♭ minor

Exercise 61: Developed Intervals in 7ths

Exercise 62: Arpeggios 5 – A♭ major / F minor

Exercise 63: Tongued Intervals in 5ths

Exercise 64: Subtone 3

Exercise 65: Expanding Chromatic 6

Lesson 15

Review Chart (page 28)

Exercise 66: Scales 8 – B major / G♯ minor

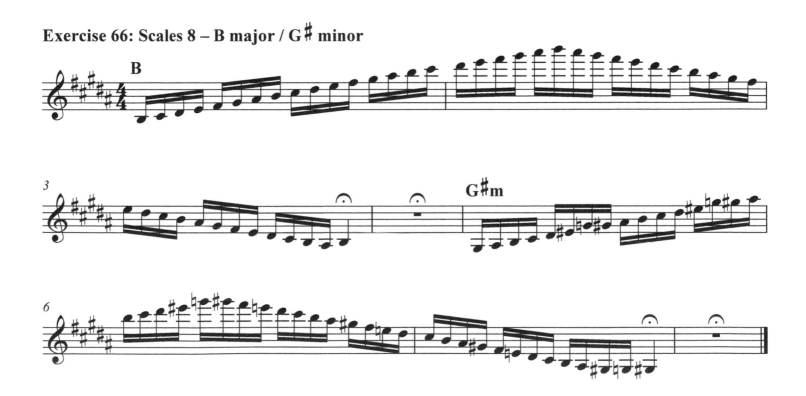

Exercise 67: Developed Intervals in Octaves

Exercise 68: Arpeggios 6 – D♭ major / B♭ minor

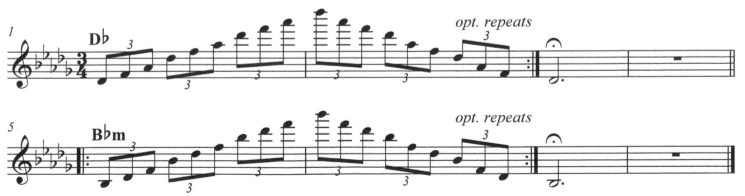

Exercise 69: Tongued Intervals in 6ths

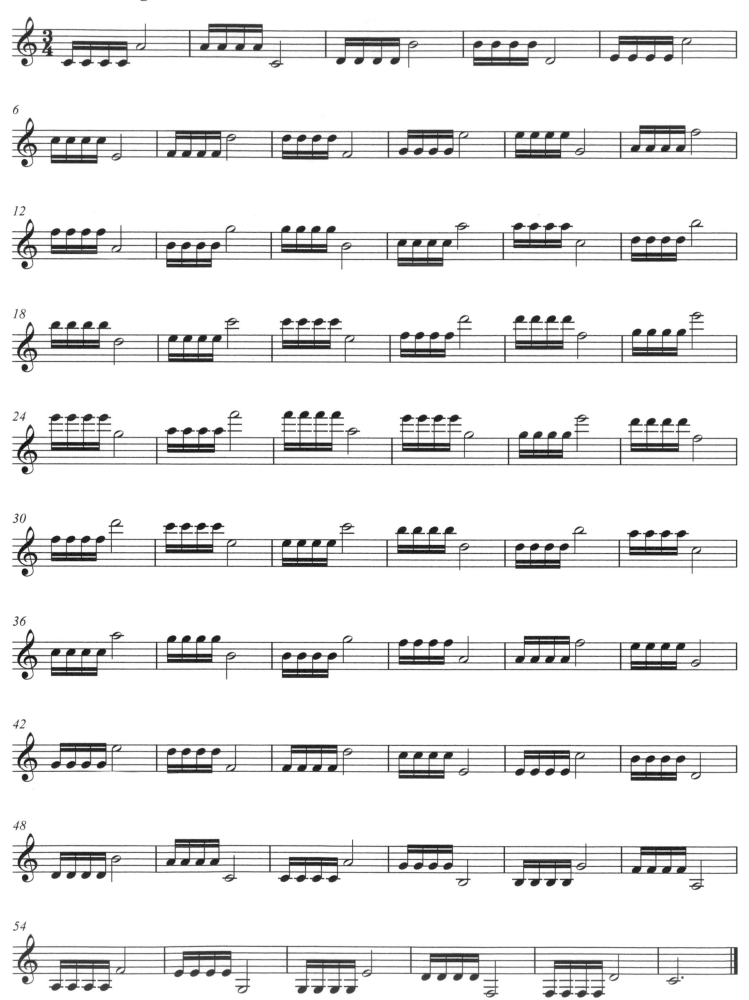

Exercise 70: Subtone 4

pppppp

Exercise 71: Expanding Chromatic 7

Lesson 16

Review Chart, then choose one Developed Interval and all other Exercises.

Exercise 72: Scales 9 – E major / C# minor

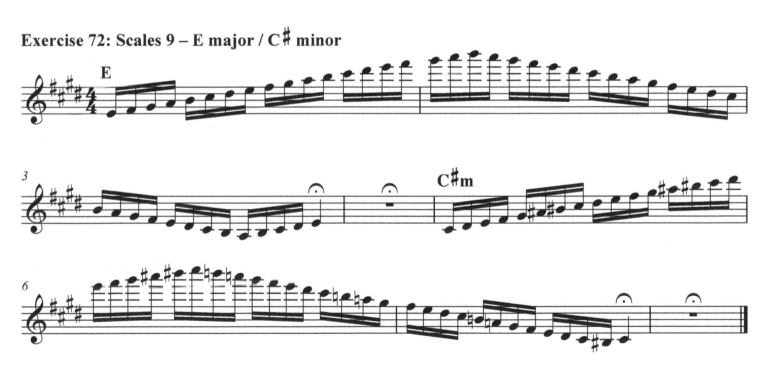

Exercise 73: Arpeggios 7 – G♭ major / E♭ minor

Exercise 74: Tongued Intervals in 7ths

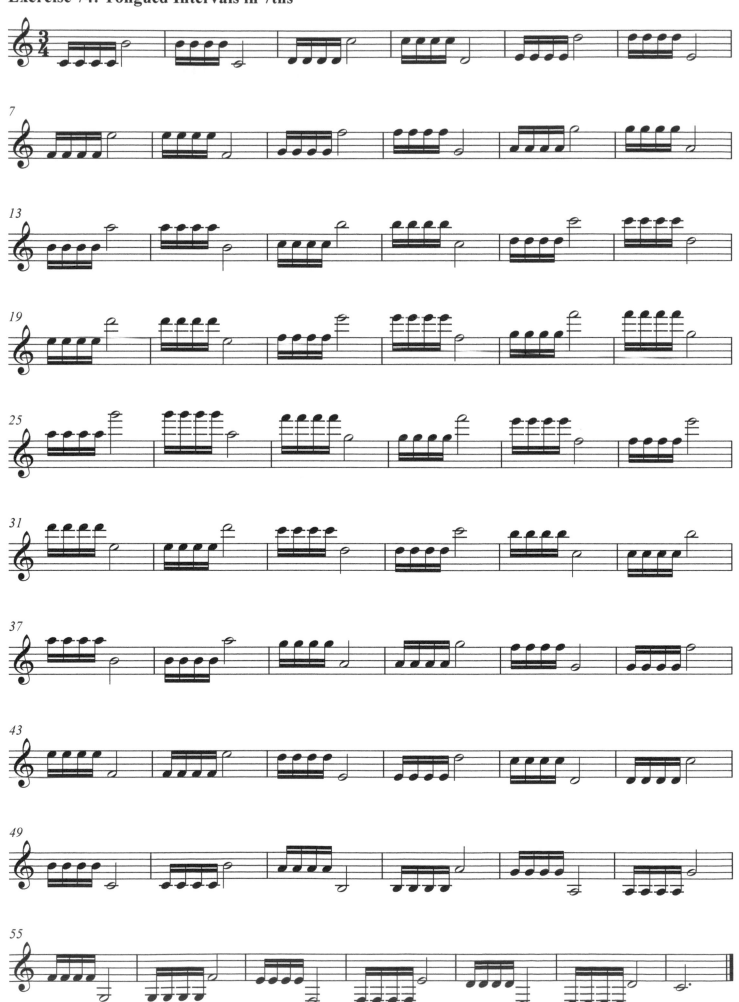

Exercise 75: Subtone 5

Exercise 76: Expanding Chromatic 8

Lesson 17

Follow **Review Chart** from Lesson 16.

Exercise 77: Scales 10 – A major / F♯ minor

Exercise 78: Arpeggios 8 – B major / G♯ minor

Exercise 79: Tongued Intervals in Octaves

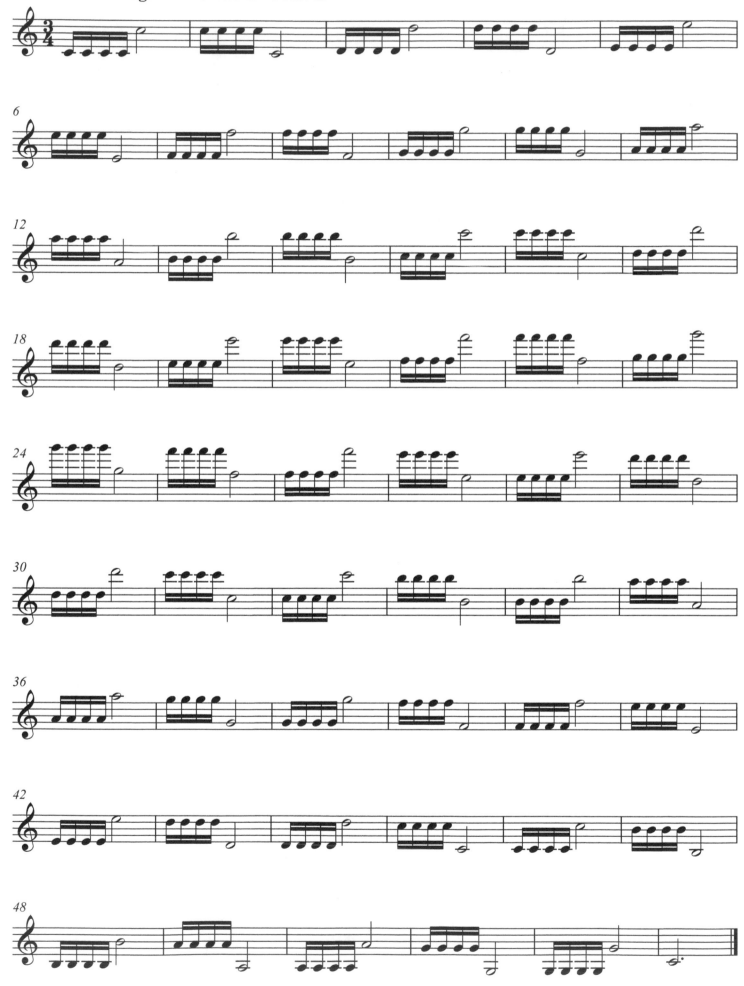

Exercise 80: Subtone 6

pppppp

Exercise 81: Expanding Chromatic 9

Lesson 18

Play:
Exercise 1: Six Notes
1 Regular Interval
Exercise 3: Harmonics
1 SLS Interval
1 Flexibility
1 LSL Interval
Pedals
1 Developed Interval
1 Flexibility
1 tongued interval
1 expanding chromatic
1 subtone

Exercise 82: Scales 11 – D major / B minor

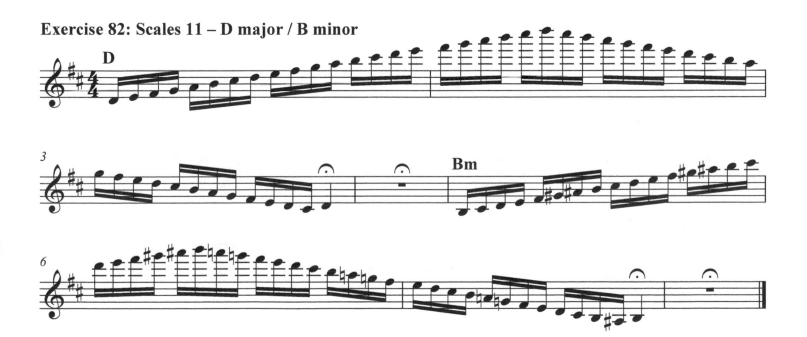

Exercise 83: Arpeggios 9 – E major / C♯ minor

Exercise 84: Scales 12 – G major / E minor

Exercise 85: Arpeggios 10 – A major / F♯ minor

Exercise 86: Arpeggios 11 – D major / B minor

Exercise 87 : Arpeggios 12 – G major / E minor

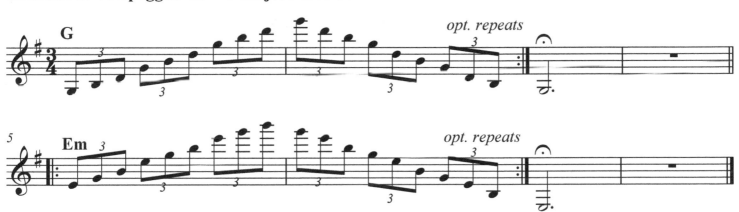

A FINAL WORD

In what I call Part 2 of my studying with Carmine, beyond MCFB, I went on to playing all the exercises you have seen in this book. In addition to those, Mr. Caruso had me practicing out of the Bettoney-Baermann method for clarinet. (See example below.)

The challenge here, of course, was the range. Isn't it always? (This example goes from low E to double high C.)

Based on my studies with Zen master Carmine and the self-discoveries I subsequently made in playing the trumpet, as well as in other parts of my life, I have adapted these findings to a way of practicing the Arban book. This approach, as well as a detailed road map to MCFB, is the focus of another book I am writing. To close this book, I leave you with these words from the Master himself, in a hand-written note he left to me.

To the Aspiring Musician:

All practice is not music. It is physical workouts. If you don't work out with the exercises you will not limber you muscles so that they become flexible. This practice will allow the muscles to move to the smallest subdivision of time. The immediacy of the muscular movement becomes the desired result. Freedom of movements (muscular) are what allows you to emote freely. I.E. the Ballerina, the Golfer, the Tennis Player, Football player. All of these above depend on muscular immediacy, which is due to the synchronization of all muscles involved in the time demand. In all games the practice of the disciplining of sensitivity (accuracy of movement) is the goal which is done by the repeated action of the muscular need until the accuracy becomes the result.

–Carmine Caruso

Thanks to Christopher Scanlon and Hugo Moreno
for their invaluable support and help in putting this book together.

ABOUT THE AUTHOR

Internationally renowned trumpet player, **Dominic Derasse** was born in France. After studying trumpet and conducting at the Nice (France) Conservatory and graduating in 1976, he was given charge of the Municipal Concert/Marching Band in St. Paul De Vence. The following year he won the competition to enter the Paris National Conservatory and graduated with First Prize in 1979.

Since moving to New York, he has performed with the New York Philharmonic, Orchestra of St. Luke's, New York Pops, American Symphony, Manhattan Philharmonic, Bronx Arts Ensemble, Colonial Symphony, Sainte Cecelia Orchestra, Naumberg Orchestra, Musica Sacra, Collegiate Chorale, New York Choral Society and the EOS Ensemble. He is in demand all over the world and has performed in Europe, South Africa, Asia, North and South America

His many recordings include *The Music of Peter Gunn* and *Sketches of Spain* with Harmonie Ensemble NY, four recordings for EOS including the Grammy-nominated Celluloid Copland, Philip Smith's *New York Legends, Music of John Corigliano* and *Music of Henryk Gorecki* with I Fiamminghi, *The Music of Ben Johnston* with Music Amici, plus numerous Broadway cast recordings and performances including *An American in Paris, Rodgers & Hammerstein's Cinderella, The Mystery of Edwin Drood, South Pacific, Assassins, Into the Woods, Kiss Me Kate*, and *Jerome Robbins' Broadway*, to name a few. He has performed on the soundtracks for such films as *Fargo* and *Beauty & the Beast* (both Oscar-winning scores), featured soloist on *Mission to Mars* and the following blockbusters: *Batman Forever, Interview with the Vampire, Ed Wood, Cobb, It Could Happen to You, Carlito's Way, The Hudsucker Proxy, Age of Innocence, Sleepless in Seattle, Muppet's Christmas Carol, Prelude to a Kiss, This Boy's Life, Lethal Weapon III, Cape Fear, Shining Through, Billy Bathgate, Barton Fink*, and many more.

Other notable solo appearances include being the guest soloist on piccolo trumpet with L'Orchestre de la Garde Republicaine for the world premiere of *Trois Peintures du Musee D'Orsay* by Eric Ewazen. Trumpet and Organ recitals at the Cathedral Saint Louis Des Invalides as well as many other venues, and Carnegie Hall's Making Music Series: H.K. Gruber. "3 MOB pieces" for Trumpet and Ensemble. He has performed Bach's Brandenburg Concerto No. 2 on four continents, founded the Aramis Chamber Orchestra, and was featured in a 31-concerts tour of Japan. His CD *Baroque Masterpieces for Trumpet and Organ* is on the Roven Records label. He also founded the *Film*harmonic Brass and produced their CD of the film music of John Williams, to be released on Roven Records in 2017.

Derasse is widely recognized in the popular music fields having recorded over 70 movie soundtracks, many TV themes including *NBC Nightly News*, commercials for over 100 products as well as live performances with Sting, Elton John, Tony Bennett, Chaka Kahn, and numerous others.

His teaching career includes a private studio, as well as master classes and clinics (based on the Carmine Caruso Technique). He recently started **System D**, a non-music-specific company. More info on Dominic and System D can be found online at *www.dominicderasse.com* and *www.systemD.biz.*

TESTIMONIALS

Unfortunately, I never had the honor or the pleasure of meeting Mr. Carmine Caruso. I knew of him only through my friend and colleague Dominic in the 1980s while we spent our evenings playing for the Folies Bergère show in Paris. In some very trying moments of my professional life, Dominic, thanks to his knowledge of the Caruso Method and pedagogy, was able to help me correct some problems I was having with my trumpet playing. He enabled me to modify my approach to the instrument, allowing me to continue on a musical career spanning another 30+ years in excellent condition.

I therefore have the utmost admiration and deepest respect for Mr. Caruso. As a trumpet player, musician, and human being, I am forever grateful.

–Guy Bardet, Paris, France, 1981

Unlike many who have studied the Caruso method and/or are writing testimonials for this book, I'm a part-time amateur player. Studying Caruso with Dominic raised my playing to the next level and allowed me to perform alongside full-time professional players with confidence. In many cases, I out-performed them. What I've found is that the Caruso Method isn't just physical calisthenics, it's also mental and emotional calisthenics. It improved my confidence tremendously and allowed me to break down many mental barriers that had been holding back my playing ability. The demands of my family life and day gig often require me to be off the horn for weeks or months at a time. My Caruso training allows me to bone-up for an important gig or rehearsal in a relatively short period of time – sometimes a week or less, if necessary.

–Gene Boyle Ridgewood, New Jersey, 2002

Using the Caruso Method as a way to address fundamental practice has been invaluable to my musical development. The exercises he developed and the mindfulness he encourages are a bedrock of my practice and my teaching, and I encourage their continued translation to new generations of brass students.

–Micah Killion, 2010
United States Air Force Band

For several years, South Carolina Low Country students and teachers were privileged to attend clinics given by Dominic Derasse utilizing his approach to the Carmine Caruso Method. As a public school educator for over 20 years and a trumpet player over 30 years, I can say without hesitation that when practiced correctly this method will build brass chops. I hit notes I have never hit in my career and felt the strength and accuracy the Caruso method builds. Thank you again, Dominic, for enlightening our students and teachers.

–Ronnie Ward, Charleston, South Carolina, 2012

Studying the Caruso method with Dominic Derasse changed my trumpet playing – and my life. After completing the course under his guidance, I now feel as if I could play or do anything. I jokingly like to tell my colleagues. "Don't study this method. You're going to improve too much and take all the gigs!" The telltale sign of a master is that she or he makes the difficult simple. For me, the Caruso Method as taught by Mr. Derasse epitomizes this idea. Thank you for this gift, Carmine and Dominic.

–Hugo Moreno, New York, 2014

Learning Caruso's pedagogy via studying with Dominic has found me playing at a new personal best. I came from a lifelong background of the Louis Maggio routine, and while I may revisit that here and there, I didn't realize how much I could benefit from Caruso's exercises and approach. It allows me to warm up much quicker, saving chops for the important stuff, and has opened up my sound in the upper register.

–Alex Bender, New York City, 2014

Dominic Derasse is one of the most in-demand trumpet players in New York City for a reason: He can play anything. Whether Stravinsky or Strayhorn, he's your man. His unreal ability to play in multiple styles at the highest level is only a testament to Caruso's revolutionary method. I think about Dominic's playing every time I pick up the horn and am happy to have learned the Caruso method from someone who studied with the man extensively.

–Evan Honse, New York, 2014

Studying the Caruso method with Dominic Derasse gave me the consistency to trust my chops and focus on the music. Although my first trumpet teacher gave me Caruso exercises as a kid, it wasn't until I met Dominic that I truly began to understand Caruso;s teachings and how to implement them successfully into my playing. His guidance gave me a routine that trains the mind and body to respond reliably and feel ready to play anything. When taught by a thoughtful teacher like Dominic who had studied extensively and directly with Carmine, all kinds of brass players can benefit from Caruso, from orchestral to commercial and everything in between. Thank you, Dominic and Carmine.

–Christopher Scanlon, New York City, 2015

I was first introduced to the ideas of Carmine Caruso in 2000 through Laurie Frink. Incorporating these concepts changed the way I play trumpet and the way I think about playing and making music. As I keep using these concepts in my daily practice, they continue to be of benefit. Working with Dominic has helped me to gain new insight and understanding.

–Bill Simenson, Minneapolis, 2015

Dominic's teachings don't just explain the Caruso method in an easy-to-digest format, but help make a connection between the body and the instrument. I saw immediate improvements in my range, flexibility, and tone once starting the Caruso exercises under Dominic's guidance.

–Dan Wendelken, New York, 2015

I have been lucky enough to hear and/or perform with Dominic in a wide variety of musical settings. I am continually amazed at how adept he is at sounding phenomenal across such a range of styles. Upon picking his brain about his musical journey and how he has developed such great balance on the instrument, he cited his decades-long application of the exercises he learned from Mr. Caruso. This volume of exercises continues those already available in print and offers us a continued succession of exercises to discover how to play the instrument in a more efficient and balanced manner. Thank you for making this invaluable resource available.

–Michael Blutman, New York, 2016